Money Sense

Consumer Sense

Andrew Einspruch

A+

This edition first published in 2012 in the United States of America by Smart Apple Media.
All rights reserved. No part of this book may be reproduced in any form or by any means
without written permission from the publisher.

Smart Apple Media
P.O. Box 3263
Mankato, MN, 56002

First published in 2011 by
MACMILLAN EDUCATION AUSTRALIA PTY LTD
15–19 Claremont St, South Yarra, Australia 3141

Visit our web site at www.macmillan.com.au or go directly to www.macmillanlibrary.com.au

Associated companies and representatives throughout the world.

Copyright text © Macmillan Publishers Australia 2011

Library of Congress Cataloging-in-Publication Data has been applied for

Publisher: Carmel Heron
Commissioning Editor: Niki Horin
Managing Editor: Vanessa Lanaway
Editors: Tim Clarke and Kirstie Innes-Will
Proofreader: Georgina Garner
Designer (cover and text): Kerri Wilson
Page layout: Kerri Wilson
Photo research: Elizabeth Sim (management: Debbie Gallagher)
Illustrator: Chris Dent
Production Controller: Vanessa Johnson

Manufactured in China by Macmillan Production (Asia) Ltd.
Kwun Tong, Kowloon, Hong Kong
Supplier Code: CP March 2011

Acknowledgments
The author and the publisher are grateful to the following for permission to reproduce copyright material:

Front cover photograph: Shutterstock/Diamond_Images, (background), /Bianda Ahmad Hisham, (background), /dibrova, (coins), /Richard Laschon, (tag), /Thomas M Perkins, (girl), /Jorge Salcedo, (background).

Back cover photograph: Shutterstock/dibrova, (coins), /Bianda Ahmad Hisham, (background), /Diamond_Images, (background).

Corbis/Blend Images/Moxie Productions, **10** (bottom), /Simon Jarratt, **13** (bottom), /Ramin Talaie, **27** (bottom), /Tetra Images, **9** (right); Dreamstime.com/Roman Ivaschenko, **21** (left), /Monkey Business Images, **6**;Getty/DAJ, **29**, /fStop Images, **11**; iStockphoto.com/Laurent davoust, **3** (top), **30** (top), /Jodi Jacobson, **18** (bottom), /Aldo Murillo, **24** (bottom), /robertas narkus, **3** (bottom), **7** (bottom), /sandsun, **21** (right), **31**, /ShaneKato, **23**; MEA/Liz Sim, **14**, **15**, **25** (bottom); Myer Pty Ltd, **16** (left); Photolibrary/Jean-Pierre Copitet, **26**, /GIRAL -, **5**, /MIXA Co. Ltd., **22**; Run Scotty Run, www.runscottyrun.com.au, **16** (right); Shopbot.com.au, **24** (top); Shutterstock/Diamond_Images, **throughout** (background), /dibrova, **3**, /Elena Elisseeva, **8**, **28**, /Elnur, **32**, /Gelpi, **4**, /Bianda Ahmad Hisham, **throughout** (background), /ard Laschon, **30** (bottom), /Lipsky, **9** (bottom), **10** (top), **12** (top left), **13** (top), **18** (top), **25** (top), **27** (top), /Lizard, **7** (top), /Robyn Mackenzie, **9** (left); Telecommunications Industry Ombudsman, www.tio.com.au, **12** (top right).

While every care has been taken to trace and acknowledge copyright, the publisher tenders their apologies for any accidental infringement where copyright has proved untraceable. They would be pleased to come to a suitable arrangement with the rightful owner in each case.

Please note
At the time of printing, the Internet addresses appearing in this book were correct. Owing to the dynamic nature of the Internet, however, we cannot guarantee that all these addresses will remain correct.

Contents

Money Sense — 4

Consumer Sense — 5

Needs and Wants — 6

Consumer Rights and Responsibilities — 10

Advertising and Consumer Behavior — 14

Handling Peer Pressure — 18

Getting the Most Out of Money — 20

Being a Smart Shopper — 22

Choosing Not to Consume — 26

Having Good Consumer Sense — 28

Find Out More — 30

Glossary — 31

Index — 32

Glossary Words

When a word is printed in **bold**, you can look up its meaning in the Glossary on page 31.

Money Sense

Money — it makes sense to know about it. People use money and think about it every day. How much money does this cost? Do I have enough money to buy that? Should I save my money for something? All of the answers to these questions relate to understanding how money works.

Money Matters

Like it or not, money matters. It matters whether people have a lot of money or just a little. How much money people have and how they manage their money both affect the life choices they can make. A decision today, such as saving money or spending it, can affect what they can do months and years from now.

> There's enough on this planet for everyone's needs but not for everyone's greed.
>
> Mahatma Gandhi, former Indian political leader

Asking yourself "What does having money let me do?" can help you develop good money sense.

Consumer Sense

Consumers are people who buy **goods** and **services**. Being a smart consumer means making the most of your money by making thoughtful decisions about what to buy.

You Are a Consumer

We are all consumers. Any time you buy anything, you are a consumer. If you make a phone call, you are consuming telephone services. If you watch television, you are a consumer of television shows and **advertisements**. When you go to the dentist, you are also a consumer, since you use the dentist's services and pay for them. Any time that we make decisions about consuming goods and services, it is important to use consumer sense.

Having consumer sense means thinking carefully about what you buy.

Needs and Wants

People consume goods and services for many reasons. It is important to understand the difference between consuming to meet a need and consuming to meet a want.

Understanding Needs

Needs are things people must have to survive or to live happy and healthy lives. People need food, water, and shelter. They also need education, clothing, and health care. Of course, not everything they need can be bought. Love, respect, happiness, and a sense of purpose are not available to buy.

Understanding Wants

Wants are things that people do not need to survive. They are nice to have, but not necessary. A new pair of designer shoes, the latest cell phone, and a faster computer are usually wants, not needs.

Food, water, and shelter are needs because they are things people need to survive.

Is It a Need or a Want?

The line between needs and wants is not always clear. Do you need that new pair of athletic shoes or do you just want them?

If all of your other shoes have holes in them, you may need to buy a new pair of athletic shoes to keep your feet dry. However, if you are buying the latest, most expensive pair because all your friends are as well, the athletic shoes are probably more of a want than a need.

Wants and Needs Change Over Time

People's wants and needs change as they grow older. A computer that was a want when a person was younger may become a need if the person works in programming or web site design when he or she is older.

To determine whether you want or need a product, such as a new pair of athletic shoes, ask yourself why you need or want it.

I need this pair for sports …

…but I want this pair because they're gold!

7

Managing Needs and Wants

Having consumer sense means being able to tell wants from needs and deciding which to meet first. Most importantly, needs must be met before wants. If people do not have enough food and water, there is no sense in them buying movie tickets! Once people have met their needs, they can turn their attention to their wants.

Most people have many more wants than they have the money to satisfy. So, they must organize them in order of importance. Sometimes a person might choose to satisfy a small want right away, such as buying a chocolate bar. At other times the person might save his or her money over time to meet a want that costs more, such as a new bike.

People should only seek to satisfy their wants, such as buying a new bag, once their needs have been satisfied first.

Compulsive Shopping

Compulsive shopping means repeatedly shopping for things you do not need, until you run out of money. It is an addiction that results from not knowing how to manage wants and needs.

Compulsive shoppers buy things in an attempt to make themselves feel better. When they are shopping, they feel good. However, this good feeling usually fades quickly. Compulsive shoppers then feel the need to keep shopping to feel good again. They end up with lots of things they do not need.

CONSUMER FACT
Around 5 percent of people are compulsive shoppers.

Avoiding Compulsive Shopping

To avoid compulsive shopping, use a shopping list and stick to it. Use **cash**, not **credit cards**, to buy things.

Compulsive shoppers confuse things that they want with things that they need.

Consumer Rights and Responsibilities

All consumers have **rights** and **responsibilities**. To be a smart consumer, people should understand both.

Consumer Rights

When people act as consumers, they have certain rights. These rights are what they can expect from **manufacturers** and **retailers**. Consumer rights are often protected by laws.

If a consumer buys a new bike that is faulty, the manufacturer must honor the **warranty** by fixing it, replacing it, or refunding the money paid.

Consumer Rights and the Law

When consumer rights are protected by laws, it means that sellers must recognise and stand by consumer rights. Governments have agencies that enforce these laws.

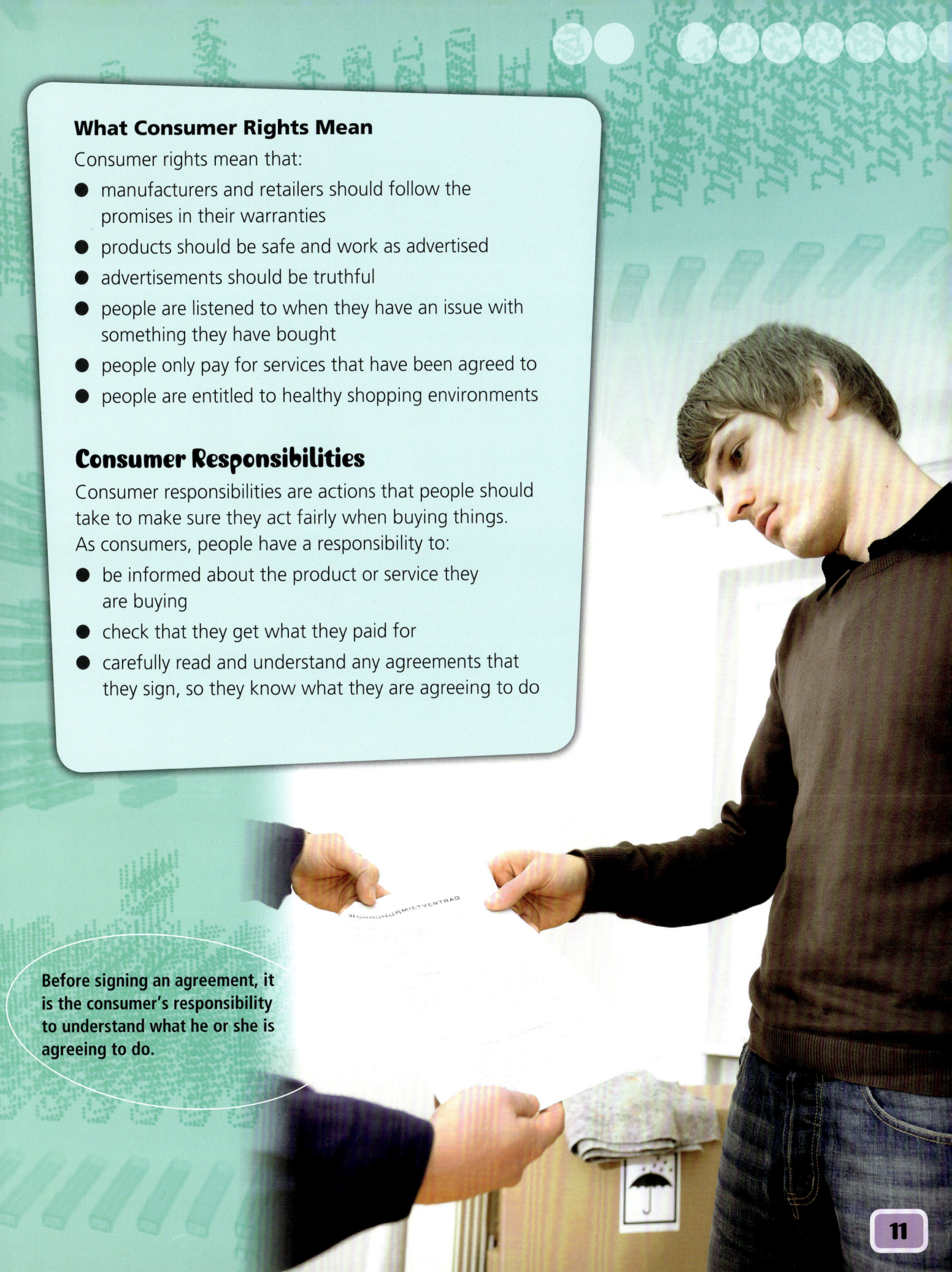

What Consumer Rights Mean

Consumer rights mean that:
- manufacturers and retailers should follow the promises in their warranties
- products should be safe and work as advertised
- advertisements should be truthful
- people are listened to when they have an issue with something they have bought
- people only pay for services that have been agreed to
- people are entitled to healthy shopping environments

Consumer Responsibilities

Consumer responsibilities are actions that people should take to make sure they act fairly when buying things. As consumers, people have a responsibility to:
- be informed about the product or service they are buying
- check that they get what they paid for
- carefully read and understand any agreements that they sign, so they know what they are agreeing to do

Before signing an agreement, it is the consumer's responsibility to understand what he or she is agreeing to do.

What Is an Ombudsman?

An ombudsman is someone who acts on complaints received about organizations. Usually appointed by the government, an ombudsman investigates an issue and tries to get the organization involved to respond to the complaint. Ombudsmen usually deal with a single industry, such as telecommunications, mining, or energy.

An important part of an ombudsman's job is to stand up for consumer rights. If someone cannot get an organization or the government to act on his or her concerns, an ombudsman can often help to resolve the matter.

Finding Out About Consumer Rights

To find out about consumer rights, search online using the terms "consumer rights," your country or state, and the area of concern, such as "banking" or "cars." The search results should help you find web sites that explain what rights you have under current laws.

Telecommunications Industry Ombudsman

Ombudsmen, such as the one for the telecommunications industry, investigate consumer complaints.

The ombudsman listens to the consumer's complaint.

The ombudsman investigates the organization whose activities have been complained about, in order to resolve the matter.

Consumer Rights Groups

Sometimes people band together to help each other be better consumers or to demand better treatment. Some consumer groups represent a particular group of people with similar interests, such as retirees, organic food growers, car buyers, or immigrants. Other groups represent consumers in general.

A group can provide information and be a voice for a group of consumers who individually may not have much of a say.

Caveat Emptor

Caveat emptor is Latin for "let the buyer beware." No matter what someone's consumer rights are, being a careful, informed consumer is the best protection a person can have.

Consumer rights groups often cover a particular area of consumer rights, such as a person's right to return clothing he or she has bought to a store, if it is faulty.

Advertising and Consumer Behavior

Advertisements are everywhere — on billboards, on television, online, even on T-shirts. Each advertisement tries to persuade people to do something or think a particular way.

The Purpose of Advertisements

The purpose of advertising is to change people's consumer behavior. Most advertisements want people to buy something, such as a particular brand of cereal or a toy. This kind of advertisement makes the product look appealing so people will want it.

Other advertisements want people to choose or follow an idea or opinion. For example, an advertisement might try to persuade people not to do something illegal, such as pirating music and movies.

Advertisements try to make products appealing so people will want to buy them.

> **In our advertising, we sell hope.**
> Charles Revson, founder of Revlon cosmetics

How Do Advertisements Persuade?

Advertisements use different ways to persuade people. Here are some of them.

Celebrities

Advertisements that feature celebrities try to tie the popularity and image of the celebrity to the product. So if a sports hero says he or she uses a particular kind of deodorant, the advertisers are hoping that the sportsperson's recommendation will help persuade people to use the same deodorant.

Emotional Appeal

Advertisements almost always appeal to people's emotions. Some advertisements try to make people feel happy, so they will associate the product with that happy feeling. Others might try to make parents feel protective, so that they will choose the product to protect their kids. Other feelings that advertisements try to stir up include excitement and desire.

Music

Music is incredibly important to advertisements because it helps create a mood. Advertisers will use different music depending on who they are aiming to persuade.

Advertisements featuring a celebrity use the celebrity's popularity to persuade people to buy something.

Images

Advertisers pay close attention to the images they use. Like music, images affect the mood of the advertisement and the emotions people feel. A soap advertisement aimed at men will have very different images from one aimed at young girls.

Laughter

Some advertisements try to get people to laugh. Laughter grabs people's attention and makes them feel good. If people like the advertisement, they will be willing to watch it more than once, which will help the advertiser reinforce its message. Making funny advertisements can be tricky, as the advertisement may only be funny once and annoying every time after that.

Which images are used in an advertisement depend on whom the advertisement is supposed to appeal to. Ask yourself: "Who are these advertisements meant to attract?"

Hundreds of Advertisements

On average, people in developed countries see between 250 and 3,000 advertisements each day.

What Can You See in This Advertisement?

Five ways to persuade you to buy the bike have been used in this advertisement. Can you spot them all?

The advertisement claims that the product is the best there is.

The product has a catchy slogan.

An offer with a time limit is used to create a sense of urgency and the need to act now.

The product is made to look as good as possible.

A celebrity spokesperson is used.

Try This: Be Advertisement-Aware

For one day (or even just a few hours) try counting every advertisement you come across. Some will be obvious, such as commercials on television or advertisements on billboards, but some advertisements are harder to spot. For example, a brand logo on a shirt counts as an advertisement.

Handling Peer Pressure

Have you ever felt like you should buy something because everyone else has one? If so, you have felt **peer pressure**.

What Is Peer Pressure?

Peer pressure is when people your age try to influence your opinions or actions. Peer pressure might be about something simple, such as buying certain clothing, or it could be about something more serious, such as skipping school.

Peer pressure is not always obvious. Sometimes it is just the feeling that you want to be like other people, or be liked by them. This feeling of peer pressure can strongly affect your consumer choices.

Good Peer Pressure

Peer pressure can be good if it encourages someone to do or buy something positive, such as choosing a product that is good for the planet.

Peer pressure can influence the kinds of phones and clothes people want to own.

How Does Peer Pressure Work?

Peer pressure can change how people feel about their wants and needs. This, in turn, can affect how they act as consumers.

Handling Peer Pressure

If you feel peer pressure, remember these tips.

- Trust your instincts — you know what is right for you.
- Sometimes the easiest way to handle peer pressure is to simply walk away.
- Arrange with your parents that if someone pressures you, you can always say, "I cannot buy (or do) that. My parents will not let me."
- If you are being pressured by your friends to make particular consumer choices, you might need to find friends who treat you with more respect.

Having inner strength is the best way to deal with peer pressure as a person and as a consumer.

Getting the Most Out of Money

It is easy to have consumer sense. People just need some common sense strategies for getting the most out of their money.

How Much Are You Spending?

The more you spend on something, the more important it is to have consumer sense. This may sound obvious, but it is worth keeping in mind. A few moments of comparing prices might be enough when you are choosing between different brands of baked beans. However, if you are spending hundreds or thousands of dollars on a computer, you should research the features and prices before you make a choice.

You need to be much more careful when making a decision about a high-price purchase, such as a computer, than for a low-price purchase, such as a comic.

> What some people mistake for the high cost of living is really the cost of living high.
>
> Doug Larson, U.S. journalist

Value for Money

Smart consumers are always looking for the best value for money. That is, they want the most benefit possible from the goods and services they buy, especially when weighed up against how much they pay. Everyone has a different idea of what represents good value. One person may value **convenience**, while someone else may look at price.

While price is important, quality matters as well. A higher priced item that is made well and will last a long time can easily provide more value for money than a less expensive, less well-made alternative.

Comparing the price and quality of similar items will help consumers find the best value for their money.

Being a Smart Shopper

An important part of having consumer sense is being a smart shopper, so that you get the best value for money possible.

Why Prices Vary

Have you ever noticed how different stores offer the same item for wildly different prices? How can they get away with that?

One reason is that large chain stores can buy huge amounts of an item at one time, so they get a better deal from sellers compared to smaller businesses that can only buy small amounts of the item. These better deals let the large businesses sell the items at a lower price.

Convenience is another reason why prices vary. Local stores that open early and stay open late provide convenience. However, these stores have to charge more for their products to cover the cost of providing that convenience.

Prices at a convenience store are usually higher because the consumer pays for the store to be open longer hours than other stores.

Buying in Season

Prices of some things vary depending on the time of year. If a fruit or vegetable is in season, there is lots of it around, so sellers lower the price to encourage consumers to buy from them and not someone else.

Buying Electronics

Electronic items usually cost the most when they first come out. If people wait to buy them, or buy the next most recent model, they can usually save money.

Shopping Around

Smart consumers shop around, especially for more expensive items. By checking more than one store, they can see who has the best deal on the goods or services they are looking for.

Buying berries when they are in season is cheaper than buying them out of season.

Using the Internet to Shop Around

The Internet makes shopping around easy. Many stores put their prices online. Sometimes people can find an item in another city at a much better price than local prices, even once they include the cost of delivery.

Some businesses only sell online, which means they do not have a physical store. Without the expense of a store, they can charge less for their products.

The Internet has made shopping around much simpler, and people can make informed decisions about what to buy.

Comparing Products Carefully

The more time a consumer spends shopping around, the more likely the person is to find the thing he or she wants for a good price. However, the person has to look closely. Many things look the same on the surface, but are really very different.

Computers are a good example. Two computers may look the same on the outside, but one may be able to do much more than the other.

Supermarkets Make It Easy to Compare

Many supermarkets now show consumers how much different products cost per a certain amount, such as 1 pound (454 g). People can compare the information on tags on shelves to see which product is better value.

For example, someone can compare a 2-pound (907-g) bag of muesli with a 5-pound (2,268-g) bag by looking at the shelf tag to compare the price per 1 pound (454 g) for each product.

No-brand Products

"No-brand" or generic products usually do not use advertising and therefore can be sold at lower prices. Sometimes these "No-brand" or generic products are exactly the same as other brands of the same product.

Supermarket tags often show how much different products cost for a common unit of measure, such as 1 pound (454 g). This makes it easy to compare similiar products.

Choosing Not to Consume

Just because people can **consume** does not mean they should. Creating goods uses up Earth's resources. Therefore, consuming for the sake of consuming is not good for the planet.

Sustainable Consumer Choices

Sometimes the best consumer choice is not consuming at all. For humans to live on Earth in a **sustainable** way, they have to use the planet's resources wisely. Too often people buy things they do not really need, or which break too soon. Think of all the cheap plastic toys that are given away with fast food meals, as well as the containers those meals come in. This is very wasteful.

People throw away so much rubbish that garbage dumps are overflowing. If people choose not to consume, fewer things need to be produced, which saves Earth's resources.

Fighting Consumerism

Consumerism is the habit of consuming. Anti-consumerism groups promote the idea that people should not be consuming so much. These groups encourage people to shop for their needs, but to limit their wants so that they buy fewer things. Anti-consumerism groups educate people about the real cost of consumer behavior, asking them to consider whether or not they really need to buy so much.

Buy Nothing Day

Buy Nothing Day, run by an anti-consumerism group called Adbusters, encourages people to choose not to consume so much and to live more simply. Their key message is that humans should consume less if they want life to be sustainable.

These people are part of an anti-consumerism movement encouraging people to consume less.

Having Good Consumer Sense

All people are consumers, so having good consumer sense and being a smart consumer should be an important part of our lives.

What Is a Smart Consumer?

A smart consumer is someone who has good consumer sense, with enough information to make sensible buying choices. These informed choices balance the person's wants against his or her needs, and are made after careful consideration instead of on **impulse**. Smart consumers avoid purchasing things for emotional reasons or because they are influenced by advertisements or peer pressure.

A smart consumer carefully considers his or her purchases.

Are You a Smart Consumer?

There is no single perfect way to be a smart consumer. You know yourself well enough to understand what you need, what you want, how you feel, and what kind of consumer you want to be. You should make consumer decisions that are right for you.

The smarter you are as a consumer, the more likely it is that you will enjoy your life. Embracing ideas such as shopping around to get good value for money can make you a better consumer than you were before.

Smart Consumer Checklist
- ✓ Do your research
- ✓ Balance price and quality
- ✓ Avoid buying on impulse
- ✓ Read your contracts, including the fine print
- ✓ Shop around
- ✓ Buy from businesses you trust

Being a smart consumer can be as simple as understanding what you need when you enter a store and only buying what you need.

Find Out More

The more people can learn about how to be smart consumers, the better their money sense will be.

Searching the Internet

If you have a consumer problem, the Internet is a great place to get information that might help you. Use your favorite search engine to search for "consumer rights," "consumer advice," "consumer complaints," or "consumer problems." You can add a location, such as your country or state, to your search — for example, "consumer complaints Arizona." You can also search for products you want more information about, such as "computers," "cameras," or "cell phones."

Web Sites

http://pbskids.org/dontbuyit/

The Don't Buy It web site helps you get smart about the media, including advertising. Have a look at the sections on "advertising tricks," and "buying smart."

www.adbusters.org/campaigns/bnd

The Adbusters web site gives information about Buy Nothing Day, an annual event to raise awareness about the need for people to consume less.

Places to Visit

The Mall

Take a trip to the mall and practice being a smart consumer. Ask yourself:
- How is advertising used?
- How can I get the best value for money for a particular item?
- How do different stores encourage me to buy their products?
- How do different stores appeal to different kinds of consumers, such as young and old, male and female?

Glossary

advertisements
forms of communication, such as notices and signs, designed to attract attention in order to sell something

cash
coins and banknotes

compulsive
unable to stop

consumers
people who buy and use goods and services

consumerism
the habit of buying and using goods and services

convenience
ease of use

credit cards
plastic cards that allow the holder to make a purchase and then pay back the card issuer later

goods
things that people can buy and touch

impulse
doing something without giving the decision much thought

manufacturers
people or companies that make things

peer pressure
the influence that people of your own age have on your opinions and actions

responsibilities
actions that people in society should take

retailers
people or companies that sell things in stores

rights
freedoms that all people in society should have

services
things that people do for other people

sustainable
able to continue so that future generations have the same choices

warranty
guarantee from a seller that a product or service will perform as promised when sold

Index

A
advertising 5, 11, 14–17, 25, 28, 30

B
Buy Nothing Day 27, 30

C
celebrities 15, 17
comparing 20, 22, 24, 25
compulsive shopping 9
consumerism 27
consumer responsibilities 10–11
consumer rights 10–12, 30
consumer rights groups 13
convenience 21, 22

E
emotional appeals in advertising 15

F
fighting consumerism 27

G
goods 5, 6, 21, 23, 26

I
images in advertising 16
Internet 24, 30

L
laughter in advertising 16
laws 10, 12

M
malls 30
money sense 4, 30
music in advertising 15, 16

N
needs 4, 6, 7, 8, 9, 19, 27, 28, 29
"no-brand" or generic products 25

O
ombudsmen 12

P
peer pressure 18–19, 28
prices 20, 21, 22, 23, 24, 25, 29

S
seasons 23
services 5, 6, 11, 21, 23
shopping 9, 11, 22–25
shopping around 23, 24, 25, 29
spending 4, 20
supermarkets 25
sustainable consumerism 26, 27

V
value for money 21, 22, 25, 29, 30

W
waiting to buy 23
wants 6, 7, 8, 9, 19, 27, 28